HAPPY BIRTHDAY

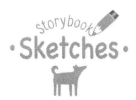

Treats

Panda

Happy Birthday

Owl

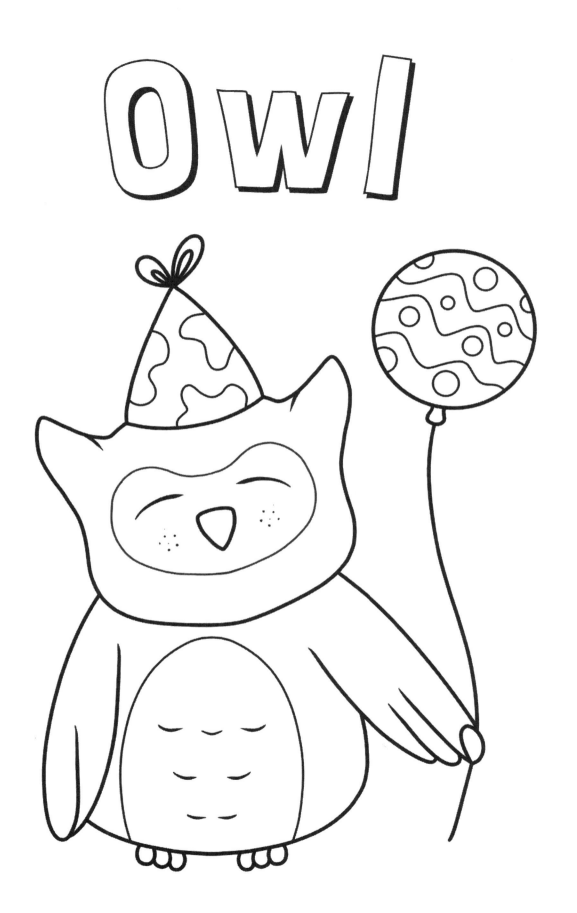

Squirrel

Koala

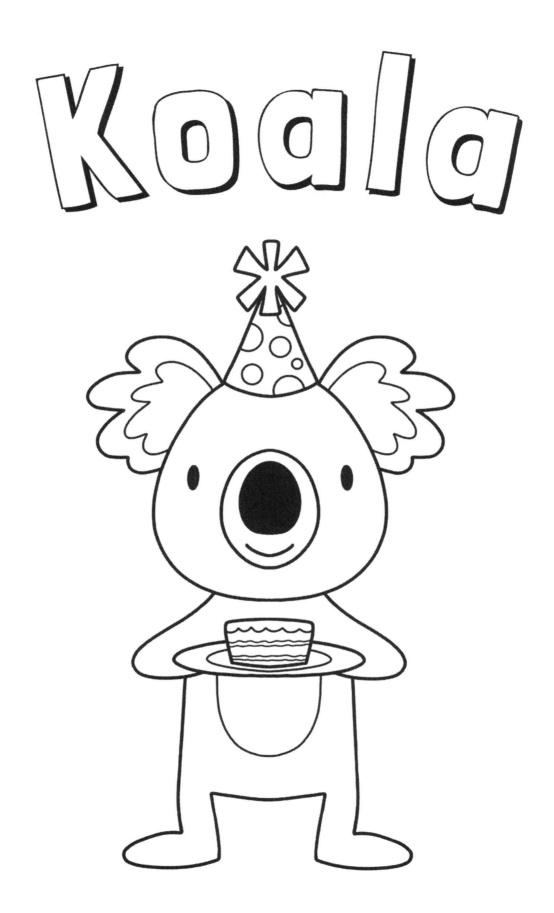

Raccoon

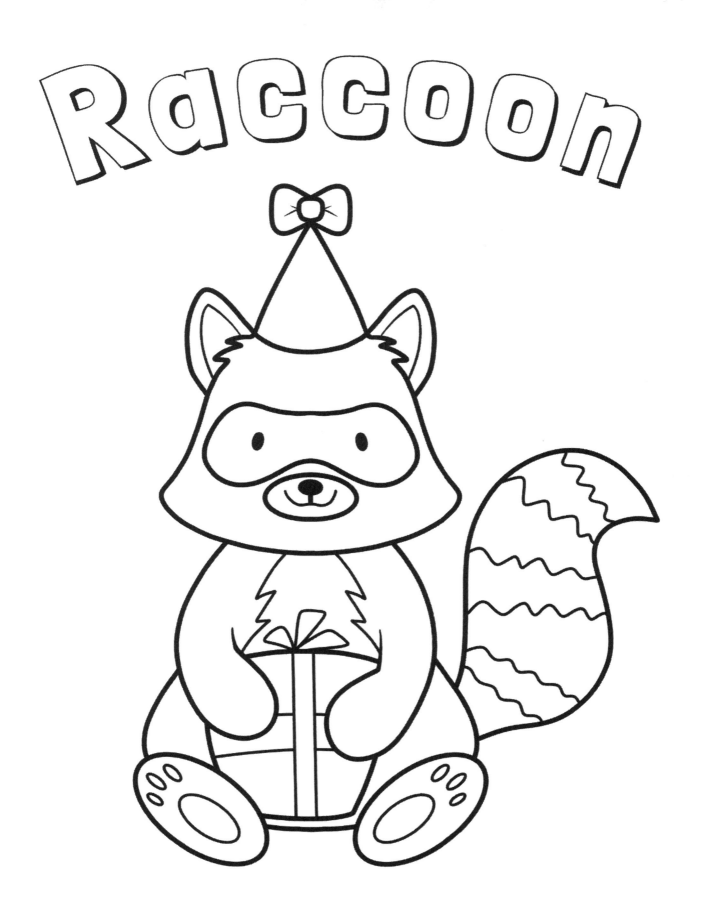

Kitty

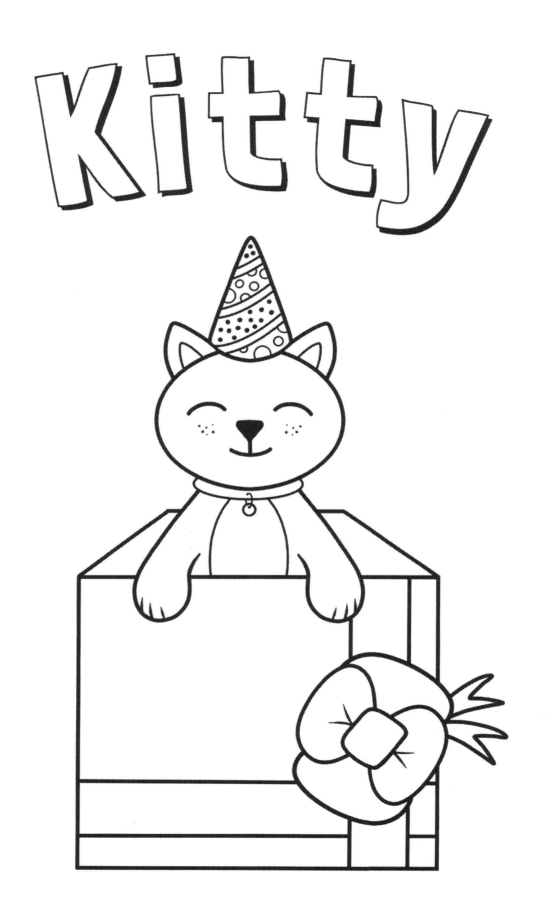

Bunny

Bear

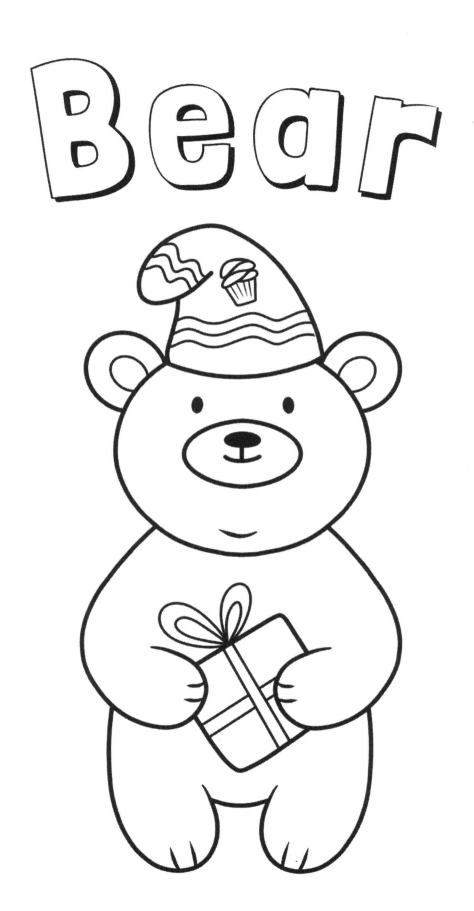

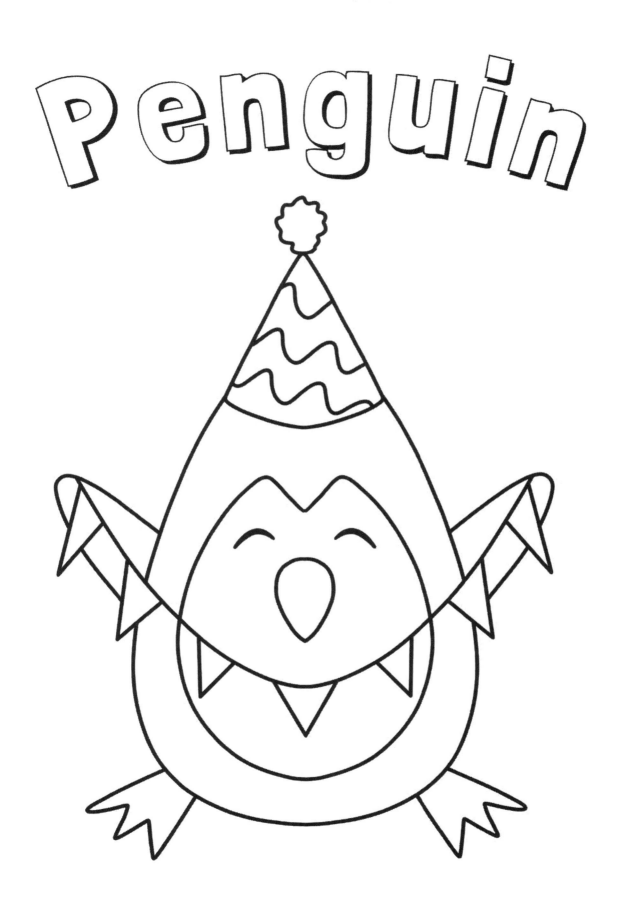

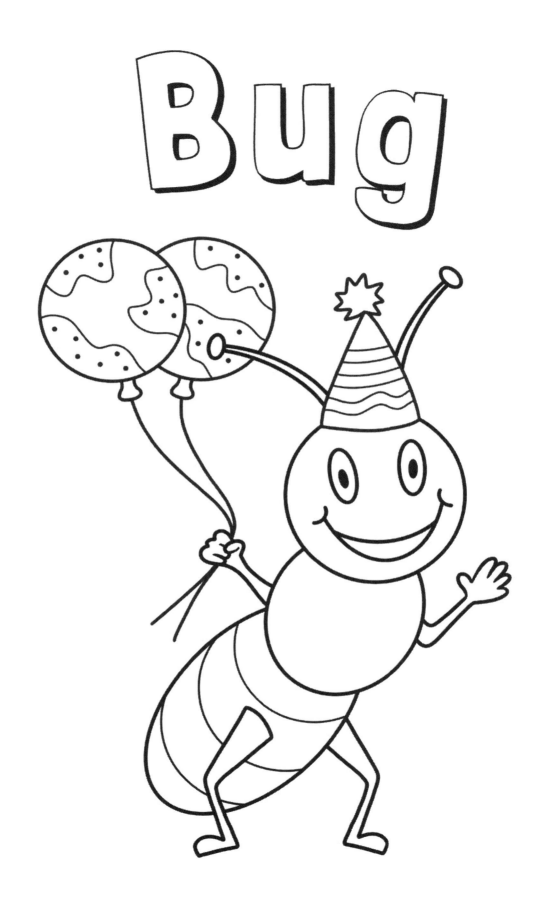

Turtle

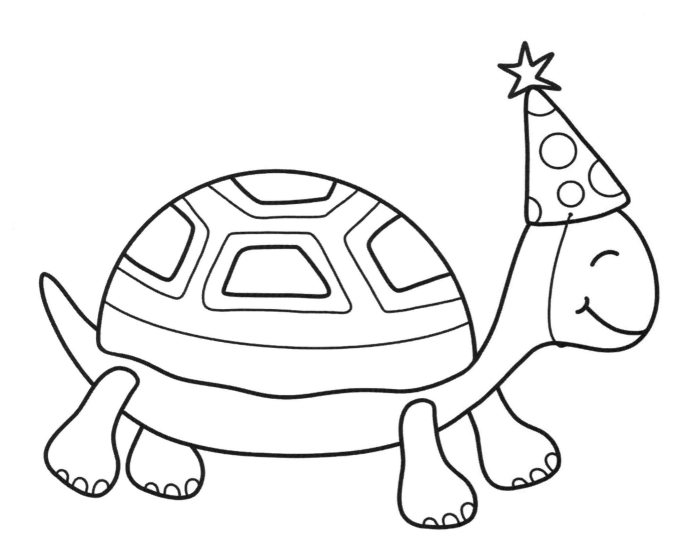

Cat

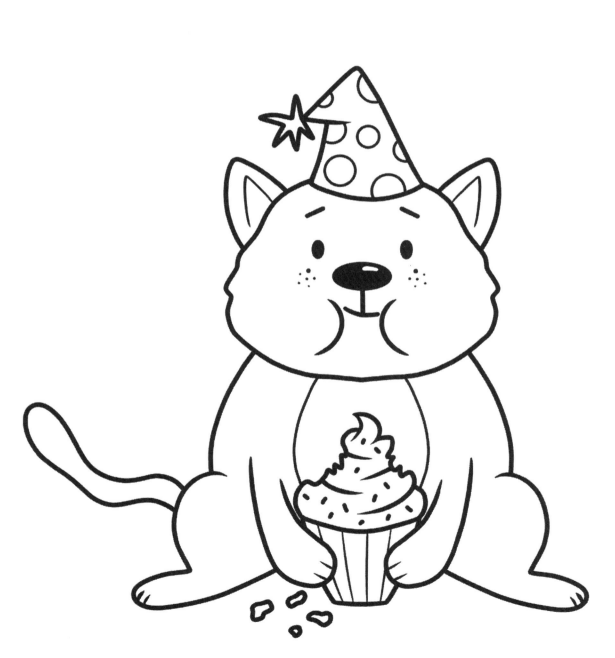

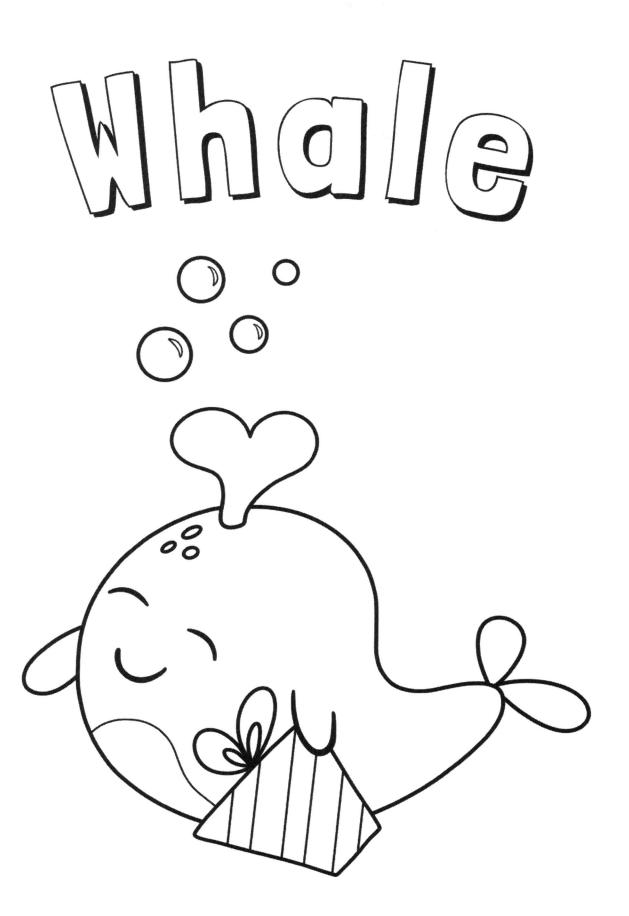

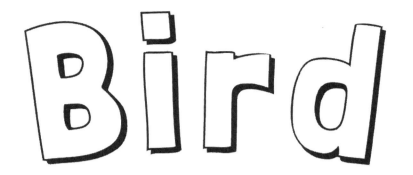

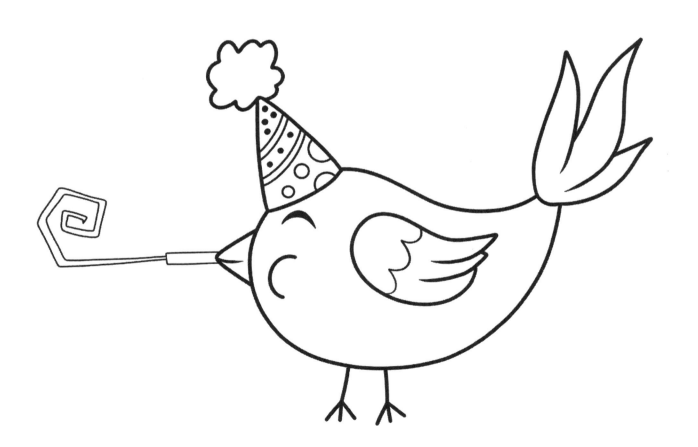

Sheep

Frog

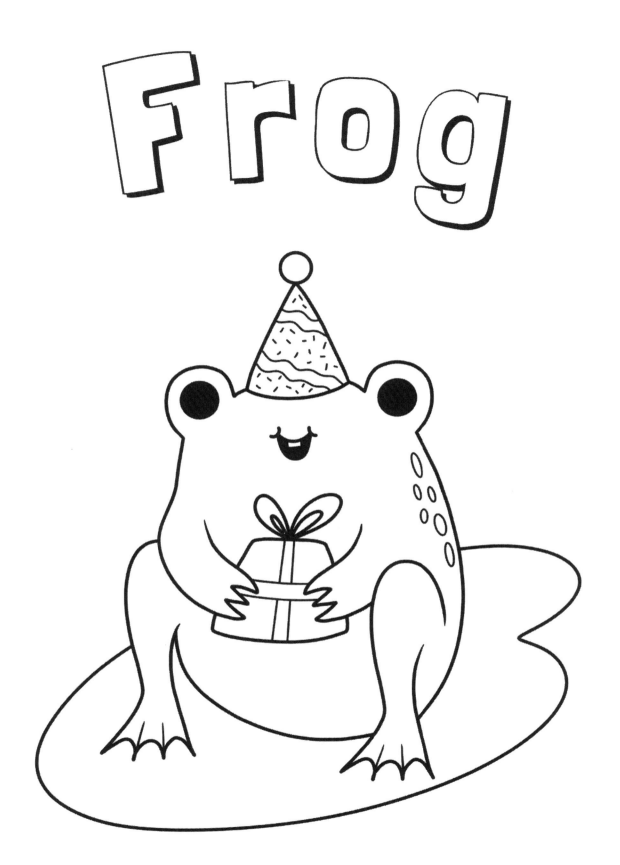

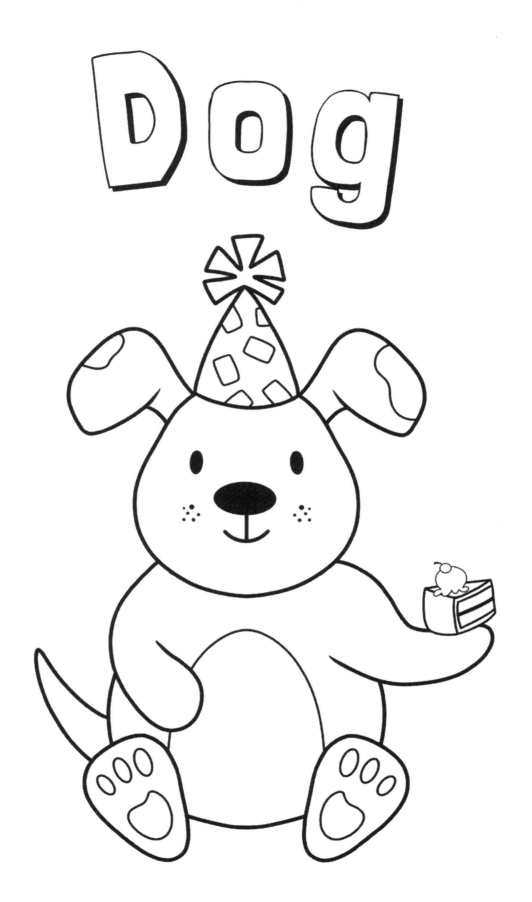

Goat

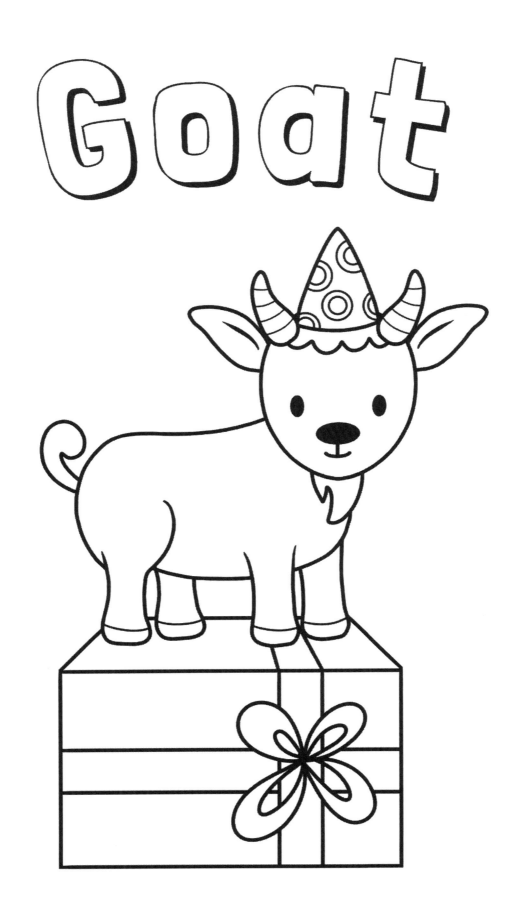

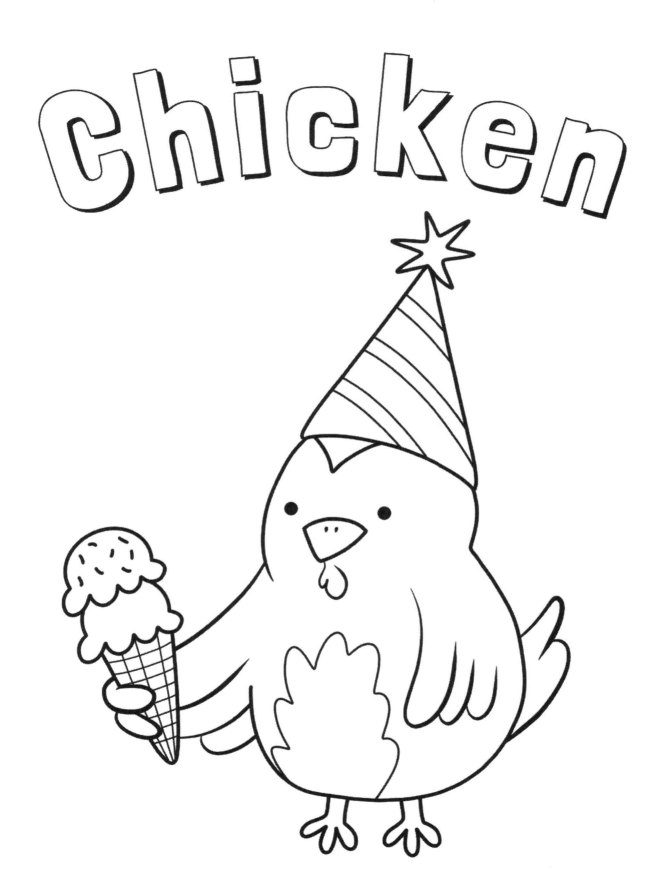

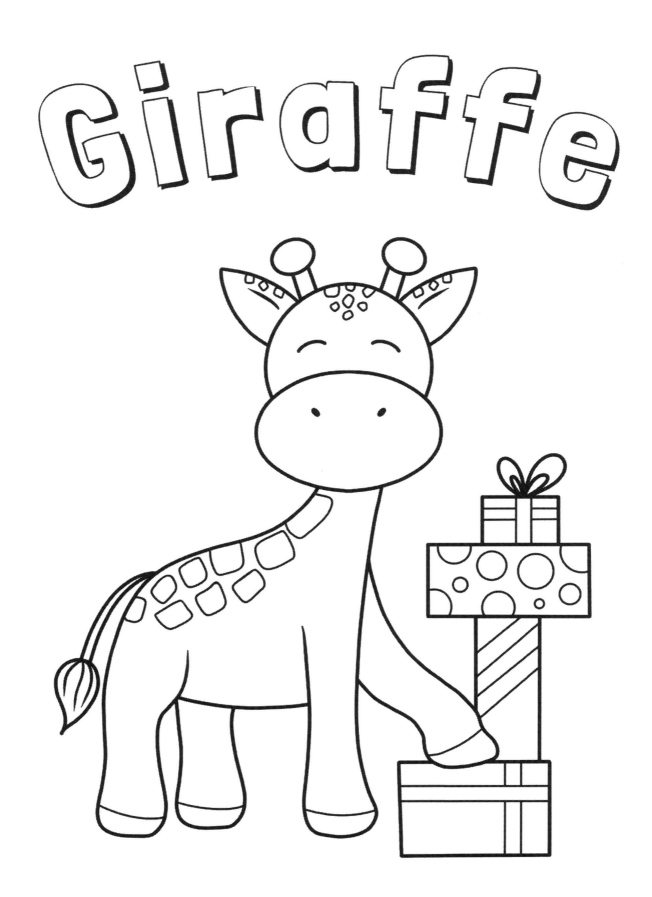

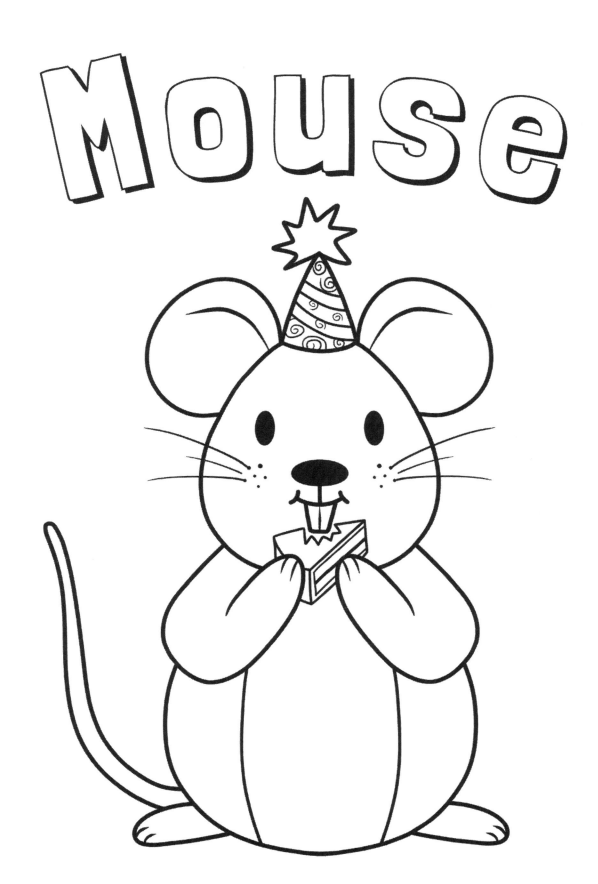

Octopus

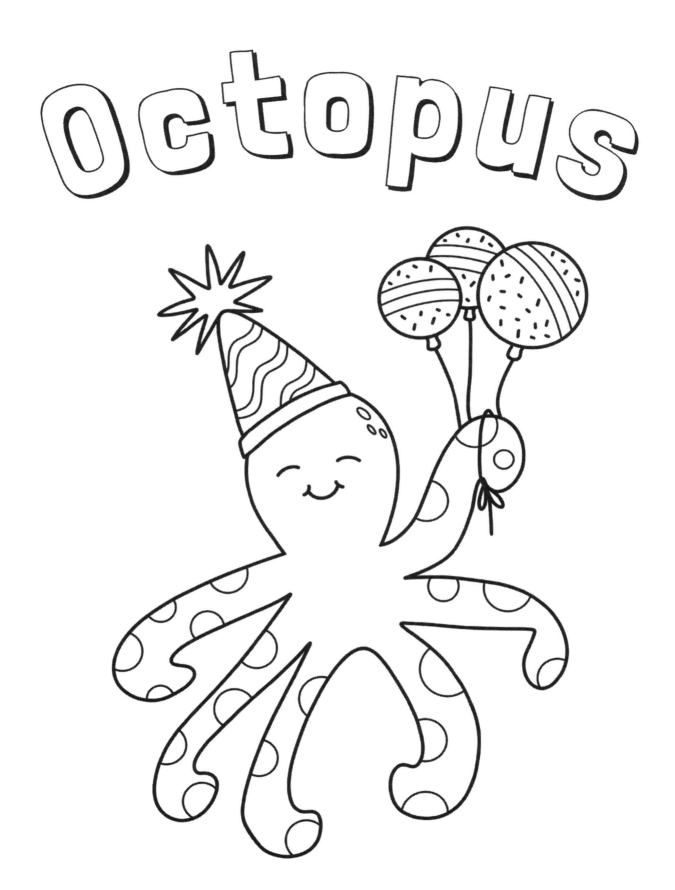

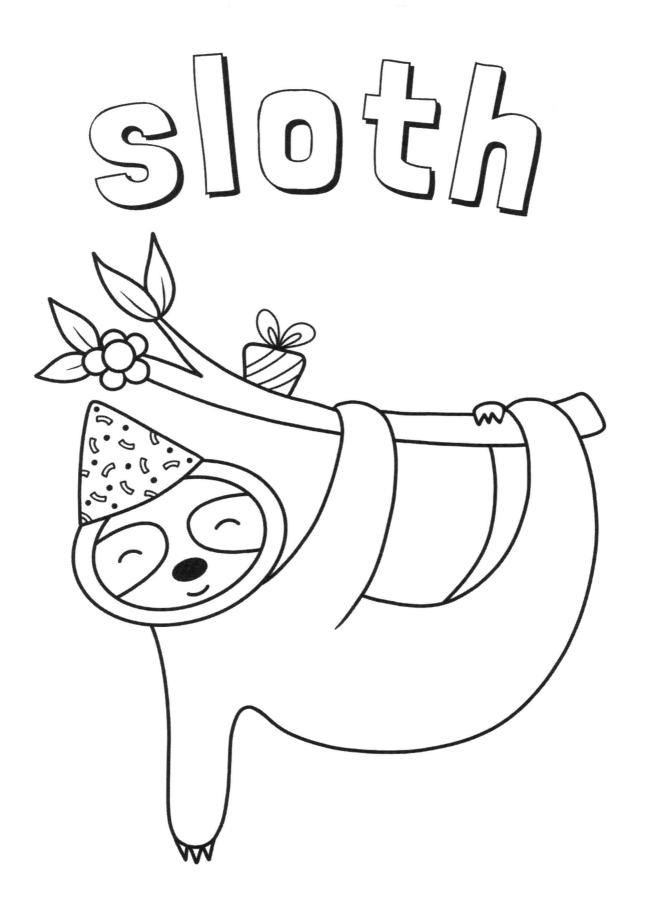

Hedgehog

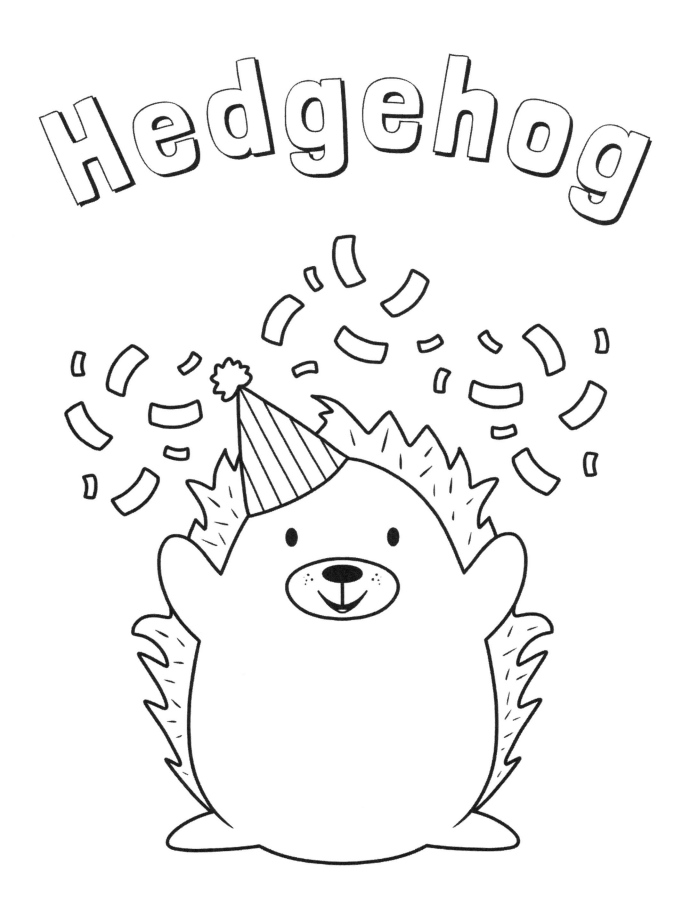

Cow

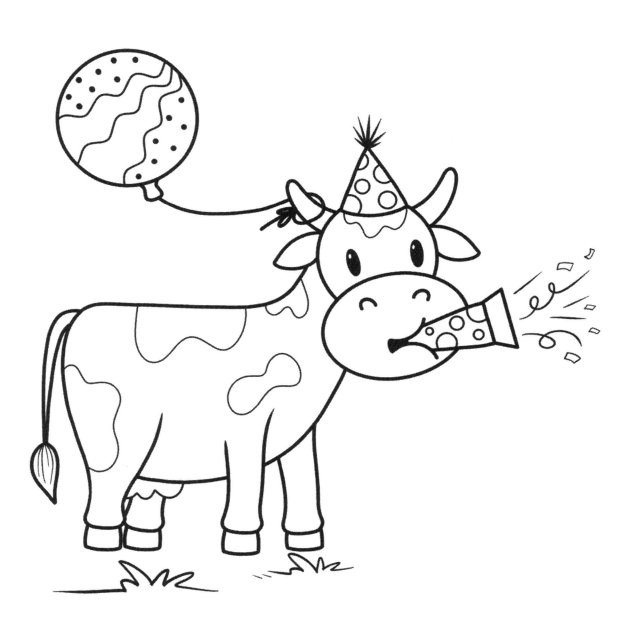

Monkey

Lion

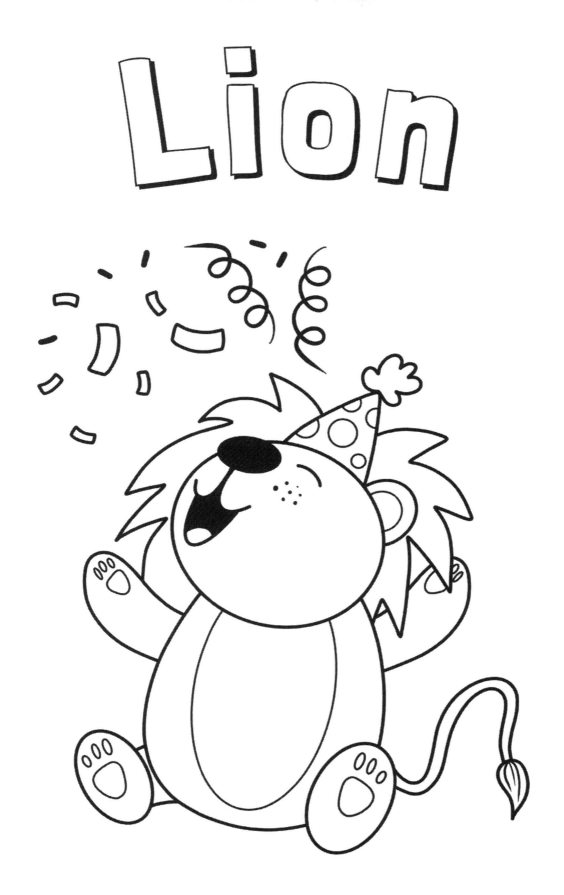

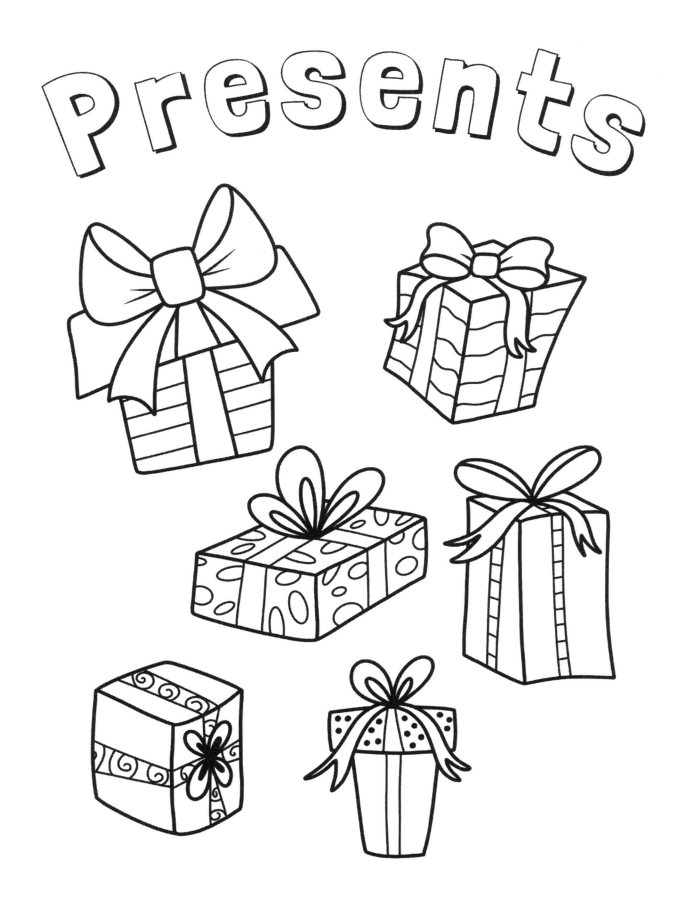

Made in the USA
Monee, IL
26 April 2022

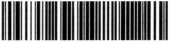

95412630R00017